Felix and Mini's Adventures

THE BIG CITY

Carolina Knight Ewing

Illustrations by Chris Ewing

Copyright 2022 © Carolina Knight Ewing Author & Chris Ewing Illustrations

All rights reserved

No part of this book may be reproduced, or stored in retrieval system, or transmitted in any form or by any means, electronic, mechanical, photocopying, recording, or otherwise, without express written permission of the copyright owner.

This is a work of fiction. The characters and events portrayed in this book are fictitious. Any similarity to real persons, living or dead, is coincidental and not intended by the author.

ISBN: 9781739689018

Cover design and Illustrations by: Chris Ewing

Printed in the United Kingdom

www.asterabooks.com

FELIX AND EVERLY'S
Mini Adventures

Books in the series

Book 1 **The Wild Garden-Spring**

Book 2 **The Big City-Summer**

Book 3 **The Old Woods-Autumn**

Book 4 **The Best Christmas (Ever)-Winter**

Follow the seasons with Felix and Everly

This one is for my Dad, for sharing his love of books and reading with me.

Contents

Chapter 1 **THE SCHOOL TRIP** 9

Chapter 2 **LOOKING FOR LUCAS** 21

Chapter 3 **TINY AGAIN** 26

Chapter 4 **IN THE BIN**..33

Chapter 5 **RISSA THE KITTIWAKE**........................39

Chapter 6 **ST JAMES' PARK** 52

Chapter 7 **THE DRESSING ROOM** 66

Chapter 8 **SQUEEZED CHEESE**...............................74

Chapter 9 **BARNEY THE DOG** 80

Chapter 10 **THE BUSY CITY**......................................87

Chapter 11 **ROOM FOR EVERYONE**.....................96

Chapter 12 **BIG TROUBLE TIME** 101

Chapter 13 **OH, NOT MUCH** 107

QUIZ TIME..122

Chapter 1
The School Trip

The July sun was blazing in the sky as Felix got on the coach with the rest of his classmates. Everly was ahead of them, sliding into a row next to her best friend who had taken the window seat.

All the kids were excited to go on a field trip for the last time that term; off to Newcastle to visit the big city.

Their trip would be Felix's last of his time at this school.

He was off to Middle School in the autumn and he was both happy and a little nervous about going. Everly said hello to her friend as the teacher counted all the children on the coach, smiling at the kids as they sat in their seats and did their seatbelts up for the hour's drive ahead. Summer was in the air and they were already in holiday mode in the last few weeks of school.

The coach turned right onto the A1, heading steadily south as the summer traffic filled the narrow road that linked England to Scotland.

They could see Lindisfarne Castle on Holy Island in the distance, one of many Northumbrian castles that dotted the coastline and countryside of the beautiful county they called home.

The children chatted excitedly and played games, passing Alnwick and then Morpeth as they made their way to Newcastle.

The coach trip was almost over before they knew it and they made their way through slow city traffic as they approached their stop, the Life Science Centre in Newcastle-Upon-Tyne.

They would spend the day exploring this science museum, getting a chance to do activities and having a picnic lunch before heading back to school at the end of the day.

The children filed into the building, 2 by 2 and holding hands with their partners as instructed. The teachers did another count to make sure no kids had been left on the coach and then they were split into smaller groups for the remainder of the day.

Felix and Everly were happy to be put in the same group. Despite being brother and sister, they still enjoyed each other's company a lot and had more fun when they were together.

They were reminded of their wild garden adventure as they approached the 'Making Studios' section of the museum where you could make your own bug hotel. It immediately made them think of Bombus and the exploits they had together in their garden.

'Felix, look!' Everly said as she pointed to the display. 'It says a bumble bee can carry up to 70 percent of its body weight.'

'Can you believe such a small creature can do that?' asked one of their teachers as he walked past them.

'I definitely can!' replied Felix as his friend Lucas giggled beside him, mucking about and giving Felix a nudge.

Everly had wandered off, keen to try out one of the displays with loads of buttons to press.

'Let's try and get away,' whispered Lucas, looking around as he tried to work out where to go if they could sneak away from the group. 'This is boring. Let's go and find something fun to do!'

'We can't!' Felix whispered back, reluctant to sneak off and get in trouble with his teacher. 'We'll get lost and the teachers will tell us off afterwards,' Felix said. He hated being in trouble.

Lucas didn't mind one bit.

'I'll just go by myself then,' Lucas grumbled as he watched the teacher walk over to the rest of the group, distracted for a moment.

Felix watched with his mouth open as Lucas darted across the room and dashed out of the door and out of sight in the blink of an eye.

'Where is he going?' asked Everly, who had been watching from a distance and seen Lucas escape.

'I'm not sure,' replied Felix. 'But I hope he doesn't get lost. He'll be in big trouble when he gets back.'

'It's his fault if he does. Lucas is always in trouble,' said Everly, disapprovingly. 'He'll be back in a minute once he realises nobody is following him,' she continued, with Felix nodding in agreement.

'You're right, he won't be away for long,' said Felix, just as their teacher beckoned the group together and started moving them along towards the door to the next room.

'But if he comes back here and we aren't in this room any longer then he will actually *be* lost,' Felix fretted, worried about his foolish friend.

'Everly, I think we'd better go and find him,' Felix suggested, looking at his little sister with pleading eyes. 'I know he's silly, but he's my friend and I want him to be safe.'

'Felix, it's a bad idea to separate from the group!' Everly replied, torn between helping her brother and doing what she was told to by the teacher. 'We'll get in trouble too!' she continued.

'If he's not back by the time we all leave this room then I think we'll have no choice,' Felix reasoned. 'We'll have to go and find him.'

They both watched with worried faces as the teacher led the way out and into the next room. Felix and Everly stayed at the back of the group and reluctantly followed as the rest of their classmates made their way to the door.

As they all filed out Lucas was nowhere to be seen, and the room was now empty apart from Felix and Everly. It was decision time.

Chapter 2

Looking for Lucas

Felix took one last glance around the room and then turned to Everly with a determined look on his face.

'I'm going to find Lucas' he said firmly. 'Will you come with me?'

'Of course I'll come with you,' Everly replied crossly. 'I don't want **both** of you to get lost. At least if we are together then I only have to worry about Lucas,' she finished, as Felix smiled at her. He could always count on her.

'OK, let's go out through that door. I hope he hasn't gone too far,' Felix pointed in the direction Lucas had left, taking a few steps towards the far side of the room.

He strode ahead as Everly followed, glancing behind her and expecting their teacher to call out their names before they'd even made it across the room.

But the call never came, and soon they were at the door and into another room. This one was huge and had other doors leading off in all directions. There was also a lift and a set of stairs.

Lucas was nowhere to be seen and could have gone in any number of rooms.

'Where do we go now?' Everly asked as Felix looked around.

'I have no idea,' Felix replied, peering up at the signs which indicated what was in each room. 'He loves Space so maybe he went to the Planetarium.'

'I guess we have to start somewhere,' Everly reasoned, starting to walk towards the door with the big Planetarium sign next to it.

Just as they were approaching the door, they heard a familiar voice ahead.

It was the other group of kids from their school with the **Head Teacher** about to lead them into the room they were in!

They'd be in big trouble if she found them walking around by themselves. And they hadn't even found Lucas yet. They couldn't risk being caught.

'Think **small!**' they both said in their heads, looking at each other and concentrating their minds together.

They'd been practising every weekend for the last 3 months, every evening after school and every morning before their parents woke up.

They were starting to master the skill of shrinking that they'd learnt that spring and now it was going to come in handy.

Very handy and in the nick of time.

Chapter 3

Tiny Again

They were tiny again.

It happened so fast they barely had time to take it all in and their heads still spun, dizzy once again but with no time to dwell on it.

Luckily, they were at the edge of the huge room already but they still tucked themselves right up against the skirting boards to avoid being trampled on.

Their teacher's enormous shoes led the way, stomping loudly as she came right past them, leading her group into the room and then through another doorway at the opposite end.

Felix and Everly stood there for a moment, taking a breath as they looked around from their new perspective.

It would take a lot longer to find Lucas if they stayed small.

'We'll have to go big again,' said Everly quietly.

'Not now!' Felix whispered urgently as another pair of feet and long adult legs walked past them. 'It's too busy here, we have to find a quiet room first.'

'How about the Planetarium? It might be dark in there,' Everly replied as she pointed to the closest door that they had been heading to and where their schoolmates had come from.

'Let's try it,' agreed Felix, making his way along the edge of the room, jumping over piles of dust and crumbs as he went.

Everly was right behind him and they quickly made their way through the open door.

They didn't get very far.

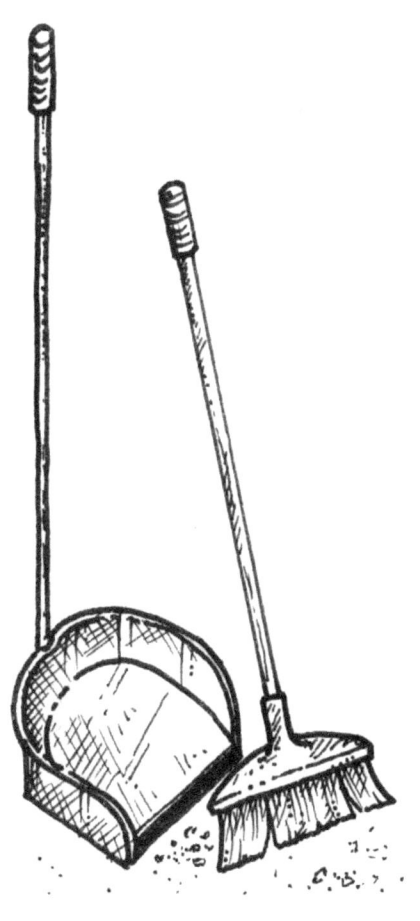

A scraping noise was the only warning they got before enormous bristles like tree branches came rushing at them and they both tucked into a tight ball to protect themselves. Thankfully, the bristles were quite soft and pushed them gently along, past the rim of a gigantic dustpan with a huge handle held by an even bigger person.

A cleaner had caught them alongside the dust, rubbish, mud and grime from visitors' shoes that had collected in the corner of the room.

They had been scooped up by a massive dustpan and broom and in one deft move they were tipped into an enormous bin.

They tumbled down with the rest of the rubbish, the cleaner absentmindedly humming to himself as he did his job, luckily not paying *any* attention to what he'd swept up.

They landed with a gentle thud on the remains of a sandwich, the soft bread cushioning their fall.

They got showered with dust as the cleaner shook the dustpan to get the last bits of dirt off it. Everly covered her head and Felix copied her, braced for a chunk of mud or something bigger that might land on them at any moment.

But the cleaner was done in that room. He grabbed the handles of the rubbish cart just out of their sight and, still humming, pushed the cart along to a lift at the edge of the Planetarium.

'I think the rubbish bag is full, lucky for us!' Felix whispered to Everly as she sat on the edge of the crust of bread, nervously looking up at the rim of the bin cart.

'I hope there's no more rubbish to come,' she said worriedly. 'We might get squashed!' she continued as the cart's wheels squeaked gently.

It came to a stop inside the lift and the cleaner pressed a button, the lift starting to descend as Felix and Everly waited nervously to find out where they'd end up.

Chapter 4

In the Bin

The sunlight gave them a hint that they'd been taken outdoors, and the cart sped up as the cleaner pushed it along to the big bins outside the Life Science Centre, ready to be tipped up.

They looked at each other in despair as they realised that they'd also end up in the big bin with the rest of the rubbish.

'We need to get out!' Everly exclaimed as Felix stood up cautiously, trying to get a better look around.

As Felix tried to reach up to peer over the edge of the rubbish cart, he heard the cleaner's footsteps moving away from them as he said hello to another member of staff who had come out of the building.

They started chatting a small distance away and Felix took his chance.

He jumped up as high as he could and made the leap onto the edge of the cart, wobbling back and forth for a few seconds before steadying himself.

'Be careful!' Everly called up. 'And give me a hand,' she continued as Felix lay down on his stomach to stretch his hand down to her.

Everly bent her knees and jumped up with all her might, grabbing onto the ledge as Felix helped her up next to him.

'We've got to get down as quickly as we can,' he said, looking at the cart and plotting the quickest route down.

Everly was already on the move, deftly finding footholds and gripping onto anything solid as she made her way down the edge of the cart.

She'd always enjoyed climbing at the play park when she was little, first it was the climbing frames and steps up to the slide and now she enjoyed the more challenging rock walls.

This was just like going down a rock wall, she told herself.

She was down in a flash.

Felix followed her just as nimbly and he quickly got to the bottom of the bin cart, stopping alongside Everly to survey his surroundings.

The cleaner's footsteps echoed around the yard as he started making his way back to his cart and, without a backward glance, Felix and Everly ran towards a nearby verge at the edge of the yard where there was the safety of the long grass to stop them being spotted.

They were safe for now. Or so they thought.

Chapter 5

Rissa the Kittiwake

Felix looked over towards the cleaner and watched as he tipped the contents of the rubbish cart into the massive bin.

He felt grateful that they'd made their escape before they ended up in there too.

He turned to Everly and said, 'We'd better find a way back into the building, but first I think it's easier if we become big again.'

'Yes, definitely,' agreed Everly. 'But we do have to watch out for the other school groups and not get caught before we return to our group. And we need to find Lucas!' she remembered, clapping her hand over her forehead.

She'd completely forgotten about Lucas and wondered if he'd had as busy a time as they'd had since he sneaked away.

'Ok, let's just wait for the cleaners to go back inside and then we can go back to being BIG. I'm sure we'll find our way back in if we go up the lift,' said Felix, carefully stepping out from the shelter of the grass to get a better view of the lift at the other end of the yard.

Just as he stuck his head out, a

GIGANTIC

beak appeared out of nowhere and grabbed his arm. Everly grabbed the other just in time as Felix got lifted clear of the grass.

Everly held onto his arm for dear life as she took a moment to realise what was happening.

A gull had picked Felix up!

Before they'd had a chance to react, the gull spread its wings and took off with Felix in its beak and Everly dangling from his other arm. Luckily, she'd managed to get a hold of Felix because he'd be long gone otherwise, without her.

'STOP! Put me down!'

'Stop!' Felix yelled over and over as loudly as he could, forgetting for a moment that the bird might not understand him using proper words.

'Felix, use your mind to talk to it!' Everly shouted back in a panic as the gull flew higher and higher in the sky. 'I'll do it too.'

'Stop!! Put us down!' they both thought at the same time, the words echoing in their heads.

The gull looked around in surprise as the words reached its head too, waving its beak from side to side as it worked out where the noise was coming from.

Felix and Everly swayed about dangerously. The gull had already left the Life Science Centre in the distance and was carrying them over busy Newcastle streets.

The noise from the traffic below made Everly pause, and she had to think quickly.

'Don't drop us!' she suddenly thought, aware of the danger they'd be in if the gull let Felix go in mid-air.

'You've got my brother in your beak,' she explained, trying to calm herself and speak clearly. 'I'm holding onto his arm and you need to land somewhere so we can get down safely,' Everly continued, hoping the gull didn't just gobble Felix up.

'Who's that speaking to me?' the gull replied curiously as it took a sharp turn over an enormous building and started its descent.

'I'm Felix, I'm the one in your beak,' said Felix, as calmly as he could.

'I think you mistook me for a worm. I'm actually a boy,' Felix continued. 'That's my sister Everly and she's not a worm either.'

The gull swooped over the edge of the huge building and dropped down in the middle of what looked like an enormous field.

It lowered its beak and gently released Felix's arm. Everly let go of his other arm with relief. Felix rubbed his arms gently to get the feeling back into them and looked up at the gull.

'I'm *so* sorry,' the gull said. 'I did indeed mistake you for a juicy worm. I did not expect to find such a tiny boy. Or girl,' it continued, turning to Everly and lowering its head.

'My name is Rissa and I'm a Kittiwake. I was feeling rather hungry. I don't eat rubbish, but I do love juicy worms and you looked just like a juicy worm. My apologies,' Rissa said, looking very sheepish for a gull.

'How on earth can we talk to each other, and how are you so small?' Rissa asked curiously.

'Well, that's a very long story,' Felix replied. 'We don't have time to go into it right now; we're on a school trip and our teachers will be looking for us soon.'

'I can take you back?' offered Rissa. 'It's the least I can do.'

Felix was about to agree to her kind offer when something caught his eye.

Peering between the blades of grass, he looked up and saw a huge, empty seating area and the distinctive black and white colours of his local football team.

'Are we in St. James' Park?' he asked excitedly, looking around the enormous stadium.

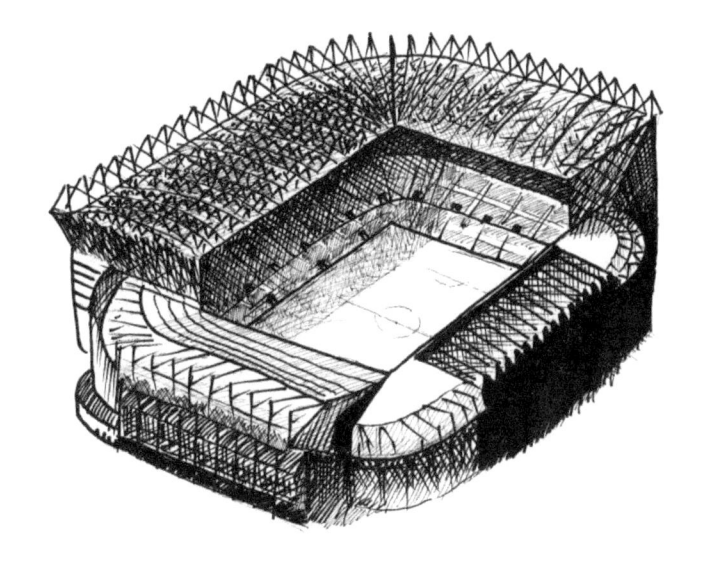

'This is the place where they kick that round thing about and run around after it, if that's what you mean,' Rissa replied. 'The other gulls all come along when all the humans are gone and eat the rubbish and food that's left behind. Us Kittiwakes don't eat old food,' she said, rather proudly.

'We like shrimps and sand-eels but they are running low at the moment. We also like juicy worms, of course,' she added, looking carefully at the grass in the hopes of spotting one.

'I can't believe we're in St James' Park!' Felix shouted in excitement. 'I've always wanted to come here,' he said. 'Everly, do you think we can stay a bit longer and look around?' he asked, turning to his sister.

Everly was torn between Rissa's offer of a lift and her brother's excited face.

'I suppose we can stay a bit longer. But I think we should go back to being big, otherwise it'll take ages to get around,' Everly reasoned.

'You're right,' Felix replied. 'Let's do it while there's nobody else here.'

'I'll keep an eye open and make sure the coast is clear,' Rissa said as she spread her enormous black tipped wings. Her beautiful dark eyes scoured the distance and she called down, 'You're good to go!'

'Think big, think big, think **BIG**!' they said over and over, just like they'd been practising all spring.

In a flash they were big once again and ready to explore.

Chapter 6

St. James' Park

'Wow.'

Felix stood in the centre of the pitch, eyes wide in disbelief as he took it all in.

'I can't believe we're on the actual football field,' he said in amazement.

'It's pretty cool,' agreed Everly, looking around at the pristine, green grass and shiny white goals at either end. 'I wonder if there's a football we can use? It would be great to have a kick-about.'

Felix ran off towards the bench and took a seat in the comfy leather seats, pretending to be a footballer.

Everly walked over to one of the goals as Rissa kept an eye from high above, swooping down every now and then.

'Felix! I've found a football!' Everly called over to her brother who was already running towards her. 'Let's take penalties!'

'You're on!' Felix replied, rubbing his hands together and jumping up and down on the spot to warm up quickly.

He took a central position in the enormous goal and Everly lined the ball up at the penalty spot which seemed miles away.

'Give it your best shot,' Felix shouted encouragingly as Everly took a run up and struck the ball with all her strength.

Despite the huge goal, she aimed it directly at Felix and he caught the ball easily, crouching down to make sure he had a good grip of it. No nutmeg for him.

'My turn,' Felix said as he ran over to the penalty spot with the ball in his hand.

Everly switched places with him and whistled like the referee starting the game.

She absolutely loved whistling.

Felix had been practising a few moves with his friends at school and wasn't going to miss an opportunity to show off his skills.

He did a dummy run and looked like he was going to kick it straight at Everly but when his foot made contact with the ball it actually curved to the edge of the goal, exactly as he'd planned it.

'GOOOAAAALLLL'

he yelled, leaping around with his arms in the air in celebration. Everly came running over to him and jumped on his back in classic footballer style.

'Ok, let's find a way inside the building,' Felix said after they'd calmed down a bit.

He ran back over to the players' bench while Everly put the football back where she'd found it.

'Everly, I think I've found the players' tunnel,' Felix called over to his sister as she made her way over to him.

'Shall we go down there?' she asked, looking around nervously to make sure nobody was watching.

'Absolutely, definitely, YES!' Felix exclaimed, beyond excited with that idea.

'Rissa, we're going inside. Don't worry about us, we'll be fine,' Everly thought as she looked up towards the Kittiwake who was flying high up towards the top stands.

'Be careful,' Rissa replied. 'I'll keep an eye out for you when you come back out,' she finished.

'OK, thanks!' Everly called back.

And with that, they took a step into the tunnel, their eyes adjusting to the different light.

'Felix, look!' Everly pointed to the walls where the words **UNITED** and **READY** were printed in huge letters with black and white pictures of players celebrating.

They walked along and up a handful of stairs, turning back to look down the tunnel and they saw

HOWAY THE LADS

written on the wall too. What an atmosphere!

Felix could almost hear the cheers of the crowd in his head, imagining being a footballer lined up with their teammates and ready to go out on the pitch. He loved football so much and being a footballer was a total dream.

He couldn't believe he was getting a sneak peek inside St. James' Park.

He got to the top of the stairs and looked round to try and spot where they might go next.

There were a few doors but one in particular caught his eye. It had the Newcastle United badge on it and he pulled Everly's arm in excitement as he ran over to it.

'I think this is the players' dressing room!' Felix was beside himself with anticipation.

'Oooh, shall we go in?' Everly asked, once again glancing around, half expecting a grown up to come marching over to them and tell them off for breaking in.

'Let's do it,' Felix replied, pushing the door open slowly in case someone was in there. The lights went on as the door opened, and there was no mistaking it.

This was definitely the Newcastle United dressing room.

Players' shirts were displayed all around the room, hanging neatly under each locker as Felix and Everly looked around.

'Saint Maximin! Trippier! Joelinton!' Felix ran all over the room, reading the names on the backs of the shirts as he went.

Everly took her time, having a good look at each and every nook and cranny, taking it all in at a slower pace.

Felix dashed about like a total daftie.

'Felix, have a look at this room,' Everly called over as she peered round a doorway.

'There's a grassy floor and a treadmill!' she described as he made his way over. It was a training room.

'Let's have a look,' said Felix, striding over to the treadmill and staring at the buttons. 'Shall we have a shot at it?' he asked with cheeky grin.

'Do you know how to start it?' Everly asked, wondering how it worked.

'Yep, Lucas has one in his house,' Felix replied as he jumped onto it and pressed a button. The machine whirred and the conveyor belt slowly started moving, picking up pace as Felix increased the speed.

He was running faster and faster now, giggling and puffing as his arms and legs moved to keep up with the pace.

Everly jumped up and down next to him, neither of them paying attention as a door closed nearby.

Voices in the room next door were the first hint they got that someone had come in.

'Felix! There's someone coming. We've got to hide!' Everly whispered and immediately said 'think *small*,' as she shrank and disappeared from view.

Felix didn't have time to stop the treadmill; he just jumped right off the end, saying 'think *small*,' mid-jump, and landed in a tiny heap at the foot of the treadmill.

Everly had hidden underneath and was waving him over furiously, the machine still moving above her head. He jumped to his feet and joined her, in the nick of time, as huge trainers and enormous legs came into view.

The footballers had arrived.

Chapter 7

The Dressing Room

Their view from under the treadmill was restricted and the only thing they could hear was the whirring of the conveyor belt right above their heads.

There were loads of legs in trainers walking around and one approached the treadmill then disappeared as the person the legs belonged to jumped onto the still moving conveyor belt.

The person must have pushed the stop button because the loud noise stopped suddenly, and they could hear voices talking to each other.

'Who was here last?' asked a man's voice right above their heads as he stepped back off the treadmill. 'It must have been someone speedy because that was quite a pace,' the man continued.

'I'm not sure,' someone in the distance replied.

'I thought we had all arrived together but I guess someone was here before us,' the first man concluded in a puzzled voice.

Felix looked at Everly and smiled, pleased that they thought he was quite speedy. He was chuffed with himself.

'I think we need to leave soon,' Everly whispered to him, bringing him back down to earth with a bump.

'You're right. We need to get to the dressing room door but that means we have to stay small. Stick to the edges and stay close,' Felix said, moving to the top end of the treadmill which was nearest the wall.

Everly followed him and they both stood near the edge where it still felt safe, taking a deep breath before breaking cover and running over to the skirting board at the wall.

Felix got a better view of the room from the corner and he gasped as he spotted a load of familiar faces from the Newcastle squad.

Some of them were warming up, others chatting, and he could hear a lot more voices in the room next door, the main dressing room.

It was a weekday, so Felix wasn't sure if they were there for a match or for training but he'd never been this close to so many footballers and he was absolutely delighted!

Everly was a bit jumpier, worried about being spotted despite being so small, and she tugged at his sleeve to get him to focus on getting out of there quickly.

Of course, nothing happens quickly when you're small.

They made slow progress around the edge of the room, moving carefully around the doorframe and into the main dressing room where, as Felix expected, most of the footballers were getting ready. It looked like they were wearing their training gear which would explain why the pitch and stadium were so quiet.

At least it also meant they had a better chance of getting out undetected.

They swerved past a pile of enormous smelly socks and kept going, their backs against the edge so they could keep an eye on any dangers coming their way.

Felix was a few steps in front of Everly and that was his big mistake.

'Watch out!'

Everly yelled as a pair of bare feet came dangerously close to Felix's head and someone sat down on the bench right above where they were walking. Humungous feet swayed above his head, one at a time, as the footballer put his shin pads, socks and trainers on. Felix held his breath and Everly looked on with wide, frightened eyes. Felix could get squashed at any moment.

It felt like a lifetime before the footballer was done and as he stood up and walked off, Felix breathed a sigh of relief.

Everly ran over to him and gave him a big hug.

'I thought you were going to get flattened!' she said with a frown. 'We really need to get out of here **NOW**.'

Felix wasn't as desperate as Everly to get going though; this was his one and only chance of seeing what went on behind the scenes and he was enjoying every minute of it.

It was worth the risk and he would cherish this moment for the rest of his life.

Chapter 8

Squeezed Cheese

The dressing room door opened and a man came in, nodding at the players and looking like the person in charge.

The room fell silent as the footballers stood to listen to what he had to say.

The room had filled with all the men from the training room too so there was an absolute sea of feet in front of Felix and Everly and they had no choice but to stay put for the moment.

Just as the manager was about to open his mouth and speak, Felix let out an absolute classic silent killer fart.

The reaction was instant.

'Ugh, that totally STINKS!' said the footballer closest to Felix, the one who had nearly trod on him. Serve him right.

'Oh man, that's a belter!' yelled another one as player after player covered their noses and backed off from the side where Felix and Everly were standing.

Felix's farts were legendary in their house, and Everly was in fits of giggles that she stifled behind her hand.

'OK, OK, settle down everyone. I think we'd best take this outside,' the manager said, opening the dressing room door and making his way out of it in a bit of a rush. The footballers didn't need telling twice, elbowing each other as they teased the player they thought was to blame for that absolutely epic squeezed cheese.

Even when tiny, Felix's farts could still clear a room.

The dressing room was empty in less than a minute and Everly burst out laughing while still covering her nose.

'Only you can fart your way out of trouble,' she said to Felix, who stood there grinning at her. 'Now I think we can give it a minute or 2 and go big so we can get out of here quickly.'

Felix agreed and took one last look around the dressing room, trying to memorise every detail.

After a good minute had passed, they both said,

'Think BIG,'

and once again they were full size and ready to cover some ground.

Everly opened the dressing room door slowly, peering out and along the corridor to check if the coast was clear.

She gave Felix a thumbs up and stepped out.

He followed her into the corridor and looked left and right to work out the quickest way to the exit. They knew that the players had made their way onto the pitch so they had to try a different route.

A big sign marked *EXIT* seemed the sensible way to go and they stepped forward cautiously, looking carefully round each doorway before heading into the next corridor.

The last room they entered had glass doors, a security desk in the corner and cabinets with busts of previous players on both sides.

Thankfully, the security desk was empty and Felix spotted the *'door release'* button in the corner near the exit. Taking one last look around, he pressed the button and the glass doors opened, fresh air spilling in.

They were out.

Chapter 9

Barney the Dog

'We need to find our way back to the Life Science Centre. We've been gone for ages and it's probably past lunchtime now,' Felix said, his tummy rumbling on cue as the hunger kicked in.

Felix was always hungry.

They walked down the stairs and towards the main road while discussing what to do next.

'Shall we try and call Rissa?' Everly asked. 'She's probably still flying over the pitch looking for us.'

'We can try and call her but I'm not sure how long our range is,' Felix replied. 'Let's give it a go anyway,' he said.

They looked up to the skies and started calling.

'Rissa, Rissa. Can you hear us?' they both called out in their minds, over and over.

'Who's that?' a new voice replied, a deeper, louder voice than Rissa's.

'I'm Felix and that's my sister Everly. Can you tell us who and *where* you are?' Felix asked cautiously, wondering who they'd made contact with now.

'I'm the chocolate Labrador dog walking along with my owner on the pavement. I'm not sure who I'm talking to or how you can hear me but my name's Barney and I'm a guide dog. Do you need any assistance?' Barney enquired.

Everly pointed to a dog a few paces away that matched Barney's description of himself. He was on a special guide dog harness, leading a girl along the pavement to the nearest traffic lights.

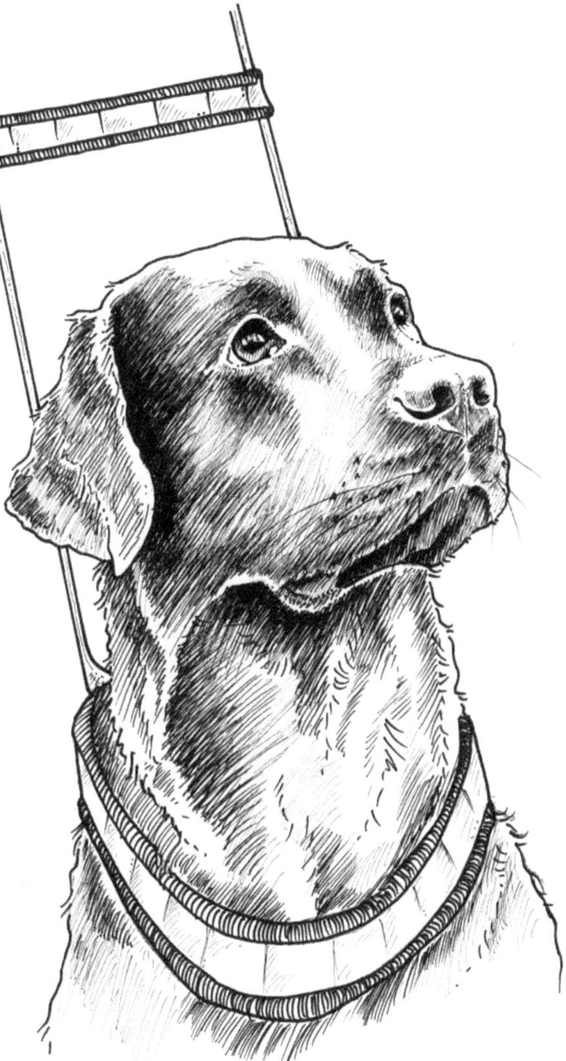

She must have been in her late teens, maybe 17 or so, and was walking purposefully behind Barney.

Felix looked at Everly and they nodded at each other.

Barney seemed friendly and, without Rissa to guide them back, they would need help finding their way around the streets of Newcastle.

They took a few steps towards Barney and he looked up, locking eyes with Felix.

'Hi,' Felix said to Barney in his head. 'Thanks for offering to help. We are a bit lost and wonder if you know the way to the Life Science Centre? We got separated from our school group and need to get back there.'

'You've made it quite a long way from the group,' said Barney. 'How did you end up all the way over here?' he asked.

'That's a bit of a long story,' Everly replied. 'But as you can see, we have an ability to speak to animals and it seems to lead us on unexpected adventures every now and then,' she explained. 'This is one of those times.'

'I see. Well, luckily for you, my owner Maisie is heading to the train station which is a skip and a hop from the Life Science Centre.

So, you can follow us and we'll lead you there,' Barney answered, sitting down as they approached the edge of the pavement, signalling to Maisie that they had to stop and wait for the green light and beeping noise before crossing the road.

'Thank you so much,' Everly said with relief. 'We'd have no idea where to go otherwise. It's very kind of you to help us.'

'I'm a guide dog,' Barney replied. 'Helping people is what I do best,' he concluded. "Now, I need to concentrate on the roads so we can cross safely. Just follow me and we'll be there in no time."

Chapter 10

The Busy City

Felix and Everly waited a few steps behind as the lights turned to amber, then red and the traffic drew to a halt.

The green man appeared on the pedestrian lights and the beeping noise indicated to Maisie that it was safe to cross, along with Barney who had stood up and started gently guiding her across the road.

Felix and Everly followed, and they all made it safely across the street. They weren't used to city life and there was noise, bustle, traffic and people everywhere.

They weaved past people walking busily along the pavement; everyone seemed to have somewhere important to go and they were all in a hurry.

Nobody seemed to have the time to look around or look up and notice a kittiwake flying high in the sky, keeping a watchful eye on the group below.

Felix was too busy concentrating on the pavement ahead, careful not to trip on loose slabs or crash into other pedestrians, trying not to drop too far behind Maisie or lose Everly in the city rush.

Everly watched in awe as Barney guided Maisie effortlessly around obstacles and dangers, a synchronised and well trained walk from both of them. Everly realized that they must have walked this path countless times to know the route in such detail.

She didn't want to distract Barney so she stayed quiet and let him do his job but she was brimming with questions. How did Maisie and Barney meet and get to know each other? How did Barney learn how to be a guide dog? Did Maisie go to high school and was Barney allowed everywhere with her? *(find out more about guide dogs on page 118!)*

She almost dropped behind the group when a grown up swept past her and briefly separated her from Felix, so she quickened her pace and told herself off for getting too distracted.

'I think we're nearly there,' Everly said to Felix as she caught up with him. 'I recognize that building up ahead.'

A large, impressive stone building was right across the street and there was a huge railway symbol that indicated it was the railway station.

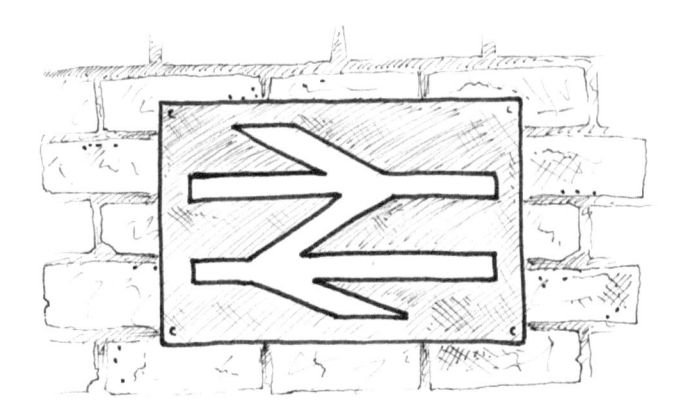

One more road to cross and they were there. Then it was just another block along to the Life Science Centre. They waited at yet another set of lights as the honk of horns filled the air, impatient drivers making their annoyance clear to everyone around as the cars filed up, stuck in traffic and *late, late, late*.

The traffic had just started moving when the lights changed for the cars once again.

The green man appeared on the pedestrian crossing lights and the beeping noise started.

It was their turn to cross.

Barney and Maisie were nearly across the street before Felix and Everly stepped out, and just as they got to the middle of the road the deafening noise of screeching tyres made them look round in a fright.

A car was coming towards them, too fast to stop and with nowhere else to go except to crash into even more people on the pavements at either side.

The driver looked at them with wide, scared eyes, realizing that the children in front of the car were in danger and just moments from disaster.

Barney and Maisie had reached the opposite pavement and Barney kept walking, almost dragging Maisie along to a safe place well away from the road edge.

'Think Small!' came the cry from high above. 'And jump on!' Rissa swooped down just as Felix and Everly shrank.

Rissa's wing almost clipped the road as she flew down at an angle to give them something to hold onto. They both jumped onto her outstretched wing as she pulled up sharply away from the car and flew them up, up, up and away from danger.

The driver of the car stepped out, looking white as a sheet. He had a mobile phone in his hand and looked dazed and confused, thinking he'd just imagined the 2 children in front of his car and the disaster that had been about to unfold.

'Felix, Everly! Are you safe?' came a distant call as Barney shouted out to them.

They were safe. Rissa had rescued them.

Chapter 11

Room for Everyone

Rissa set them down gently near the lift doors close to where she had scooped them up earlier in the day.

'Are you O.K?' she asked as they looked around in a daze. 'You're bound to be a bit shocked after that. Take a deep breath and give yourselves a moment,' Rissa said reassuringly.

'That was scary,' Felix replied, finding his words after a few moments of silence. 'I thought we were going to get hit by that car. Thank you for saving us,' he continued softly. 'We owe you our lives.'

'We can't thank you enough, Rissa,' Everly agreed, looking remarkably calm considering what they'd just been through.

'You're welcome,' Rissa replied, 'I'm just glad I was in the right place at the right time.

I'm always wary of those huge machines that you humans seem to love. They seem so dangerous to me.'

'That was enough adventure for one day. We really need to get back to our group now,' Everly said, looking around to get her bearings. 'Where will you go from here?'

'I'm heading back to my nest at the bridge.

It's the furthest from the sea that we go and has the most Kittiwakes by far. We are glad there is still room in the city for us birds, even if it is a bit tricky to find a safe place to nest with all those spikes and nets that have been put up,' Rissa replied sadly.

'The best way you can thank me is to make birds in your gardens and near your homes feel safe and welcome with plenty of nature and space for us. There's room for everyone,' Rissa finished, getting ready to set off one last time.

'We'll tell everyone all about the Kittiwakes!' Felix promised as Rissa spread her wings and took off, hovering above them as they pressed the lift button.

'Goodbye, Rissa. Thank you!' Felix said as the lift doors opened, and Rissa flew off into the distance.

'Goodbye!' came the call as she became a dot on the horizon.

They stepped into the lift and Everly reached up to press the button which said '*Ground Floor*'. The lift doors closed. They were done with the big city and ready to go back to their quiet village.

But first, they had to face the music.

Chapter 12

Big Trouble Time

The lift doors opened at exactly the same place where their adventure had started. They were in the Planetarium.

So was their group, with the teacher scratching his head and counting the children in front of him with a puzzled look on his face.

'Oh, there you are! Where have you been?' he said, with a mixture of relief and annoyance in his voice.

So, he **HAD** noticed that they were gone. Uh-oh.

'They followed me out,' Lucas piped up, sitting there among their classmates, eating his sandwich. 'When I cut my finger earlier,' he continued, lifting his hand that had a plaster on it for everyone to see.

The plaster had stars and planets on it.

'Felix, is that true?' the teacher demanded, crossing his arms and looking down sternly. 'Did you go and help Lucas find a staff member when he cut his finger?'

Felix looked over at Lucas helplessly and saw his friend nodding his head vigorously up and down, giving Felix the biggest hint to go along with his story.

'Yes, we did,' Everly chimed in, getting the message, loud and clear. 'We saw that Lucas had gone out of the room and followed him to make sure he was safe,' Everly said, grateful not to have to actually lie. They had done *almost* exactly that.

'We all went to the front desk and the staff there got the first aid kit.

But they didn't have any plasters so the lady had to go to the office to find some and it took ages and we were very bored and we sat about waiting forever, then Felix needed the toilet and Everly went with him and then we got separated and I eventually got my plaster and found you again and they must have got lost!'

Lucas was telling the most elaborate tale and he was enjoying every minute of it.

Felix just nodded in agreement as the teacher looked back and forth at them and Lucas.

'Right. Well. Well done for helping your friend,' he said rather reluctantly.

He wasn't sure whether he entirely believed the story but Lucas told a good tale. 'Next time, just come and get me first,' the teacher said firmly.

And that was that.

No telling off.

No trouble.

Felix sat down next to Lucas who had kept his packed lunch safe. 'Thanks, I owe you!' he said quietly.

'You owe me an adventure!' Lucas replied with a grin. 'You were gone for ages! What did you get up to?' he asked, curiously.

'I don't even know where to start. I'll tell you another time,' Felix replied wearily, not for the first time that day, jamming a sandwich in his mouth almost whole. He was starving.

Lucas looked at him sideways but let it go. For now. He knew Felix and Everly had been up to something and he was determined to find out what it was, eventually.

Chapter 13

Oh, Not Much

The return trip to the school was a rather quiet one. All the children were tired and ready to go home.

They arrived back almost at home time and were only in the classroom for 5 minutes before their parents arrived to collect them all.

Felix ran out of the class doors first and spotted his dad in the yard waiting to collect him and Everly.

Everly wasn't far behind Felix and they both gave Dad massive hugs, nearly flattening him.

'Hello you two! It's like I haven't seen you in years!' he teased, ruffling Felix's hair affectionately and squeezing Everly tight. 'Did you have a good day?'

'Yes, it was fun,' Everly replied as they walked towards their house carrying their packed lunches.

'Where did you go? What did you do?' their dad continued.

'Oh, not much,' said Felix casually.

'Just the usual," Everly agreed. 'This and that.'

'What was the Life Science Centre like?' Dad prodded, keen to hear more.

'It was cool,' Felix replied.

'And Newcastle? Was it fun being in the big city?' Dad wasn't giving up easily.

'It was busy. And noisy,' Everly said dismissively as they reached their house.

'Shoes off at the door. And go and wash your hands,' Dad finished, defeated by their unenthusiastic responses.

He had absolutely no idea what adventures they'd just had.

Everly looked at Felix as she washed her hands and said quietly, 'That was a bit of a crazy day, Felix.'

'I know,' he replied. 'I think I'd be happier if we just stay around here and don't get into so much trouble next time. We were lucky to get away with it.'

'Yes,' agreed Everly. 'We were very lucky.'

'There's absolutely no chance of any trouble like that around here,' said Felix.

Little did they know that their next adventure was just around the corner.

Around the corner and over the field at the end of the village, in the woods nearby.

THE END

FELIX AND EVERLY'S
Mini Adventures

Books in the series

Book 1 **The Wild Garden**
Book 2 **The Big City**
Book 3 **The Old Woods**
Book 4 **The Best Christmas (Ever)**
Love the series? Give the books a review!

Sneak peek of Book 3

The Old Woods

'The warning has been raised to a RED alert. From 3pm. That means now. We aren't taking any chances. It's pretty blowy out here already!' Dad said, bang on cue as a massive gust nearly swept Felix off his feet. His coat whipped open as he battled with the zip and his backpack flapped about in the wind.

They walked briskly home, heads down against the wind, eyes watering and their ears filled with the noisy howl and whoosh of the wind in the trees close by.

Felix was relieved to be home, closing the door with a bang against the elements, pulling his shoes off and smiling at his sister who was already sat in her onesie on the sofa near the fire.

'Felix!' she exclaimed excitedly. 'Mum says the winds are now going to be up to **70** miles per hour. I'm not sure what that means, exactly, but it sounds like a lot.'

'That's pretty windy,' Felix agreed as he sat down next to her. Storms and weather events were some of the things he liked to read about.

'Hurricane force winds are above 74 miles per hour so we aren't far off that!' he explained, as Mum and Dad busied themselves bringing extra coal and firewood indoors.

'Are we really going to have hurricane force winds?' he asked his parents, looking at them in some doubt.

'We can't be sure, Felix, but whatever happens we are as prepared as we can be. The alert changed to RED at 11am so we popped to Berwick to get some more supplies, more coal and food, batteries for the torch and candles. So, we are all set, whatever happens next,' Dad reassured them both.

'O.K, good,' Felix replied, relieved that he was only 10, after all, and the grown-ups had the boring job of worrying about things and getting prepared for events like these.

He went upstairs and quickly changed out of his uniform, straight into comfy joggers and a onesie on top to stay cosy, heading back downstairs as soon as Mum called out.

'Hot chocolate is ready!'

He was down in seconds, sitting by the fire, the telly on and a biscuit within easy reach.

They were warm, cosy and safe.

Ready for the storm.

The Old Woods is out now

in E-book and paperback.

Buy it on Amazon,

just search for Felix and Everly.

More about amazing Guide Dogs

- Guide dogs and their humans have a lot of training to learn how to work well as a team and help visually impaired people in their day to day lives.

- They have an initial 3 week training session in their home area and work or school to become good working partners and get to know each other well.
- The guide dogs association support the family and dog at each stage to make sure everyone is happy.
- After at least 5 weeks the dog and person become official partners and it takes about 12 months to really get to know each other.
- Guide dogs need daily walks, care and attention just like any other dog.
- Visually impaired kids can get guide dogs too, depending on their needs and abilities.

Source: **www.guidedogs.org.uk**

Kittiwake Facts

- Scientific name: **Rissa tridactyla**

- Bird family: **Gulls and terns**

- UK conservation status: **Red** (Endangered)

- Population: UK Breeding 380,000 pairs

- What they eat: fish, shrimps and worms.

- Kittiwakes are coastal gulls. In the breeding season, look for them at seabird colonies around the UK.

- In late summer and autumn they can be seen flying past offshore, or gathering at roosts. They spend the winter months out at sea.
Source: **www.rspb.org.uk**

- Where the River Tyne passes the quaysides between Newcastle and Gateshead you can find '**The Worlds Furthest Inland Breeding Colony of Kittiwakes in the World**'.
- They are a soft gentle Gull with friendly personalities and they wear the black and white colours of the local Geordie football team Newcastle United.
Source:**www.tynekittiwakes.org.uk**

QUIZ TIME

Wordsearch

F	H	A	F	C	E	F	W	A	T
I	A	B	O	G	X	J	G	E	E
N	L	R	Y	N	P	R	I	R	A
K	I	T	T	I	W	A	K	E	C
U	K	B	S	W	R	I	N	M	H
E	N	U	B	O	M	E	V	M	E
D	O	O	F	D	O	G	H	U	R
L	L	A	B	T	O	O	F	S	L

BIN
DOG
FART
FOOTBALL
KITTIWAKE
SUMMER
TEACHER
WING

Word Pairs

Fill the gaps and match the words

FELIX   ___A__ __ __Y

MAISIE   K_T__I W__K__

FOOTBALL   E_ __R_Y

RISSA   ___T_ D__UM

Summer Nature Trail

What can you spot in your garden or local park?

Gull   **Dog**

Foxgloves   **Poppies**

Pigeon   **Swallow**

Beetle   **Caterpillar**

Blue Tit

Add your own sightings too!

Acknowledgements

My biggest thanks go to our family, friends, community in the local area and throughout Northumberland for supporting the first book and being so encouraging to a new author.

Once again, I owe so much to Chris, my husband, illustrator and cover designer who brings the stories to life with intricate and beautiful drawings.

About the Author

Carolina Knight Ewing

Felix and Everly's Mini Adventures is my first children's book series. The first 4 stories follow the seasons and I'm working on the next book now.

I've travelled a fair bit to far flung places such as Australia, Brazil, Mozambique & Finland and will be taking Felix and Everly to all sorts of exciting destinations too.

But I started closer to home, with 'The Wild Garden' in Northumberland, followed by 'The Big City' adventure in Newcastle. The North East of England is our home and there is so much inspiration where we live.

Keep up with the latest releases and updates on **www.asterabooks.com and buy 'Felix and Everly's Mini Adventures' on Amazon now.**